Essentials of
Life Insurance

Steven M. Bragg

AccountingTools®

For more information about AccountingTools® products, visit our Web site at www.accountingtools.com.

Table of Contents

About the Author

Steven Bragg, CPA, has been the chief financial officer or controller of four companies, as well as a consulting manager at Ernst & Young. He received a master's degree in finance from Bentley College, an MBA from Babson College, and a Bachelor's degree in Economics from the University of Maine. He has been a two-time president of the Colorado Mountain Club, and is an avid alpine skier, mountain biker, and certified master diver. Mr. Bragg resides in Centennial, Colorado. He has written more than 300 books and courses, including *New Controller Guidebook, GAAP Guidebook*, and *Payroll Management*.

Steven maintains the accountingtools.com web site, which contains continuing professional education courses, the Accounting Best Practices podcast, and thousands of articles on accounting subjects.

Buy Additional AccountingTools Courses

AccountingTools offers more than 1,500 hours of CPE courses, with concentrations in accounting, auditing, finance, taxation, and ethics. Related courses that you might like include:

- Charitable Contributions Tax Guide
- Estate Planning Fundamentals
- Guide to Gift Taxes
- Guide to Individual Retirement Accounts
- Investing Guidebook

Go to accountingtools.com/cpe to view these additional courses.

AccountingTools®

Essentials of Life Insurance

Introduction

Life insurance is an insurance product that pays out a designated amount of cash upon the death of an insured person. When there are many policyholders paying for this insurance, the net effect is that the payouts triggered by policyholder deaths are paid for by the insurance premiums being paid in by the other policyholders. In effect, life insurance is designed to require a small periodic payment in exchange for a large payout at some uncertain future date.

In this manual, we discuss a broad range of life insurance issues, including how life insurance works, the types of life insurance, how much of it to acquire, useful policy riders, how to obtain a claim payout, and much more.

Types of Expenditures Requiring Life Insurance Coverage

There are many types of expenditures that can be covered by the payout from a life insurance policy. When determining how much life insurance you might need, it is worth considering which of the following expenses might apply to your situation, if you were to die:

- *College expenses.* Estimate the amount of cash your children will need to attend college. This includes tuition, room and board, study materials, and incidentals. In addition, assume that these costs will increase by at least the rate of inflation.
- *Debt payoffs.* Consider the amount of outstanding debts that will need to be paid off, including your mortgage, credit card debt, car loans, and so on. Paying them off through an insurance payout will leave your family in a much less precarious financial situation.
- *Estate taxes.* A particularly good use for life insurance is when you have a large estate that will be subject to estate taxes, and which is comprised of mostly non-liquid assets (such as your ownership interest in a business). In these cases, it may be necessary to sell the non-liquid assets quickly, in order to pay the estate taxes. To give your beneficiaries the option to retain control over your assets, it makes sense to obtain sufficient life insurance to pay the expected amount of the estate taxes.
- *Funeral expenses.* Depending on the extensiveness of the affair, a funeral can easily cost a minimum of $10,000.
- *Operational replacement.* A possible use for life insurance arises when you own a business, and it depends on you for a large part of its cash flow (perhaps because you are great at sales!). If you want the business to stay in operation after your death, consider how much additional cash it will need until a replacement for you can be found. This is also known as key person life insurance. Or, think about how much cash it will need until a buyer can be found

for the business. This should constitute the amount of life insurance you will need.

- *Readjustment period.* Your surviving spouse may need several months away from work to adjust to life as a widow/widower.
- *Survivor living expenses.* Consider the inflation-adjusted amount of cash that your surviving spouse and children will need for ongoing living expenses, including utilities, food, clothing, travel, medical needs, and so on. This amount can be reduced by your surviving spouse's estimated income.
- *Viatical settlement.* Under viatical settlements, terminally ill policy holders sell their policies for a percent of the death benefit. The buyer then becomes the new beneficiary of the policy, pays all remaining premiums, and eventually collects the death benefit. The intent behind these arrangements is to give the policy holders enough cash to support them through the remainder of their lives.

We expand upon these concepts in the next section.

How Much Life Insurance is Enough?

The amount of life insurance to include in an insurance contract will depend on the needs and financial circumstances of each person. There are a number of ways to answer this question, including the following:

Rough Calculations

- *Debt payoff.* A low-end target for life insurance is to obtain just enough to pay off your existing debts, such as your mortgage. This approach establishes a lower threshold, since it will leave your spouse with no debts, but also no reserve of cash to pay for ongoing expenses.
- *Income multiple.* A common approach is to acquire an amount of life insurance that is a multiple of your annual income. The exact amount varies, depending on who is providing the advice, but can be up to eight times your annual pay. This is an extremely rough measure, since it does not account for other factors, such as the presence of children who will need to be provided for, how much you have already saved, and how much you plan to spend each year to maintain a specific lifestyle.

More Precise Calculations

- *Human life value.* Human life value is a somewhat hazy notion, but represents your income potential over the remainder of your life. It can be calculated as an estimate of your future income over the period when your dependents will need support, discounted[1] back to its present value. This approach is more quantitatively correct, but does not take into account any special needs, such as debt payoffs or the college requirements of children. Thus, it can yield results that are somewhat low.

EXAMPLE

Blaire is 50 years old. He discusses family finances with his wife, and they conclude that the family will need at least $60,000 per year until his retirement age, which is 15 years in the future. They decide to use a 4% discount rate, which is what they currently earn on a certificate of deposit. The calculation is for the present value of an ordinary annuity of 1, for which the multiplier is 11.1184. By multiplying the $60,000 annual payment by the 11.1184 multiplier, Blaire arrives at a life insurance value of $667,104 that he will need in order to meet the family's life insurance needs.

- *Capital preservation*. This approach focuses on acquiring a sum of cash that is then invested, where your dependents live off the income generated from the insurance settlement. This approach is designed to provide a stream of income for quite an extended period of time, and so is a reasonable approach when your dependents are still young. If the presumed rate of return is relatively low, this approach will result in the largest possible life insurance requirement.

EXAMPLE

Kathryn is unmarried, with two small children. She wants enough life insurance to ensure that her children receive $50,000 per year in earnings from the life insurance payout. At a 3% assumed rate of return on invested capital, this will require her to purchase $1,666,666 of life insurance (calculated as $50,000 ÷ 3%).

- *Capital liquidation*. This approach focuses on having sufficient cash to cover the needs of your dependents for a specific period of time, after which the cash runs out. This is because the principal balance is gradually drawn down through the usage period. This approach requires less life insurance than the capital preservation approach. The main concern here is that the projected usage period is correct, since it is possible that the dependents will actually need the cash for a longer period of time. Another concern is that the actual rate of return on the principal is lower than expected.

---

[1] The discount rate used for a human life valuate calculation is typically tied to a conservative investment option, such as the rate on a money market investment or a certificate of deposit.

EXAMPLE

Scott's wife has died, leaving him with sole responsibility for two children. He wants them to have $80,000 per year until age 20, which is 10 years from now. He assumes that the rate of return on investments for the next 10 years will be 4%. At that rate of return, he will need $2,000,000 of life insurance (calculated as $80,000 ÷ 4%). Paying for that much insurance would be difficult for Scott, so he instead calculates the required amount of life insurance using the capital liquidation approach; the result is $648,872, which he can afford. The calculation is as follows:

Year	(A) Principal	(B) Interest (at 4%)	(C) Year-end Payout	(A + B – C) Ending Principal
1	$648,872	$25,955	$80,000	$594,827
2	594,827	23,793	80,000	538,620
3	538,620	21,545	80,000	480,165
4	480,165	19,207	80,000	419,371
5	419,371	16,775	80,000	356,146
6	356,146	14,246	80,000	290,392
7	290,392	11,616	80,000	222,008
8	222,008	8,880	80,000	150,888
9	150,888	6,036	80,000	76,924
10	76,924	3,077	80,000	0

- *Capital needs analysis.* This approach yields the most accurate results, because it takes many factors into account, such as presumed increases in your income through future years, future tax payments on that income, and deductions for your presumed future living expenses. The intent is to derive the net amount of positive cash flow that you would have generated over the term of the insurance contract. However, an additional analysis will be needed in case there are any lump-sum payouts required immediately following your death.

EXAMPLE

Brittany is estimating the amount of life insurance she should obtain under a capital needs analysis. In the following analysis, she assumes that her current income will increase at a rate of 4% per year, on which she will pay 20% income taxes. She also assumes $12,000 per year in medical and life insurance premiums, and that 25% of her income goes to self-maintenance expenses of various types. The resulting net balance of cash left over is then discounted to its present value, using a 3% discount rate. The result is a need for $343,966 of life insurance.

Year	Presumed Income*	Income Taxes**	Insurance Premiums	Self-Maintenance Expenses ***	Net Balance	Present Value****
1	$80,000	$16,000	$12,000	$20,000	$32,000	$31,059
2	83,200	16,640	12,000	20,800	33,760	31,822
3	86,528	17,306	12,000	21,632	35,590	32,568
4	89,989	17,998	12,000	22,497	37,494	33,313
5	93,589	18,718	12,000	23,397	39,474	34,050
6	97,332	19,466	12,000	24,333	41,533	34,784
7	101,226	20,245	12,000	25,306	43,674	35,511
8	105,275	21,055	12,000	26,319	45,901	36,324
9	109,486	21,897	12,000	27,371	48,217	36,954
10	113,865	22,773	12,000	28,466	50,626	37,671
					Total	$343,966

* 4% growth rate
** 20% income tax rate
*** Set at 25% of income
**** 3% discount rate

No matter which of these approaches is used, it is likely that the ideal amount of life insurance will change over time, due to changes in your circumstances – such as a marriage or re-marriage, more children, a change in profession, disability, and so forth. This means that your life insurance needs should be re-evaluated at regular intervals.

Another factor to consider is that the amount of life insurance you will need is likely to decline as you age, since your other assets (such as a retirement account and equity in a home) are likely to grow over time.

Expectations for Life Duration

Another issue when determining life insurance levels is how long you can reasonably expect to live. The Centers for Disease Control periodically issue an updated life expectancy table, for which an extract from the 2020 table appears in the following exhibit. These figures can worsen substantially if your family's medical history includes unusual frequencies of diabetes, heart disease, cancer, and so forth.

CDC Life Expectancy Table

Age (years)	Total	Male	Female
0	77.0	74.2	79.9
1	76.4	73.6	79.3
5	72.5	69.7	75.3
10	67.5	64.7	70.4
15	62.6	59.8	65.4
20	57.7	55.0	60.5
25	53.0	50.5	55.7
30	48.4	45.9	50.9
35	43.8	41.5	46.2
40	39.3	37.0	41.5
45	34.8	32.7	36.9
50	30.4	28.4	32.4
55	26.2	24.3	28.0
60	22.2	20.5	23.8
65	18.5	17.0	19.8
70	14.9	13.7	15.9
75	11.6	10.6	12.4
80	8.6	7.8	9.2
85	6.1	5.5	6.5
90	4.2	3.7	4.4
95	2.8	2.5	2.9
100	2.0	1.8	2.0

The Insurable Interest Concept

An *insurable interest* is an economic stake in an event for which someone purchases an insurance policy to mitigate the risk of loss. In short, in order to purchase an insurance policy, you must have more to lose than to gain through the death of the insured party. This means that every person has an insurable interest in himself, anyone on whom he depends for education or support, and anyone obliged to make payments to him. Here are several examples of parties considered to have an insurable interest:

- An employer has an insurable interest in an employee, since the employee's death might cause financial losses for the employer.
- A business has an insurable interest in an owner, if it has an arrangement to buy back the ownership interest of the owner.
- The co-owner of a home has an insurable interest in the other co-owner, if the parties are sharing the expenses of inhabiting the home.

This is an essential concept, since in the absence of an insurable interest, someone could purchase an insurance policy on another party with the intention of murdering that person and pocketing the resulting insurance payout.

Any person is considered to have an unlimited insurable interest in him or herself, and so can purchase as much life insurance as they want. Realistically, the amount of life insurance purchased will be capped by the insurer, and will also be limited by how much the policy holder can afford to pay in premiums. The insurer will want to know the reasons for any excessive amounts of life insurance, and will probably only agree to an amount that roughly matches the future value of the beneficiary's economic loss in the event of the insured party's death.

Once an insurable interest has been established and a policy purchased, it is generally possible in most states to alter the beneficiary, even if that party has no insurable interest. In addition, someone taking out a policy on his own life can make the policy payable to literally anyone, even if the designated beneficiary has no insurable interest in the policy holder.

The Beneficiary Concept

A *beneficiary* is the party that will receive the payout from your policy's death benefit when you die. The primary beneficiary is the party you select that is entitled to the policy's payout when you die. It is also possible to select a contingent beneficiary who will be next in line for the payout in case the primary beneficiary dies or cannot be located. It is possible to name multiple primary and contingent beneficiaries. A variation on the concept is to direct that, if a beneficiary were to die, the payout is to go to that party's heirs, rather than being paid to the other beneficiaries.

> **Tip:** Always identify beneficiaries as clearly as possible, including their full names and social security numbers, so that they can be readily identified for policy payouts.

In addition, a policy may designate a beneficiary as being revocable, in which case you can change the beneficiary without the consent of the current beneficiary. Conversely, if the beneficiary is irrevocable, then you must get the current beneficiary's consent before altering the beneficiary to a different party.

> **Tip:** Minors cannot be named as direct beneficiaries, so you may want to create a trust in the child's name or designate an adult custodian who can be named as the primary beneficiary, and who will then administer the funds on behalf of the minor.

A life insurance payout goes directly to the designated beneficiary, avoiding the delays of the probate process.

The Life Insurance Underwriting Process

Life insurance underwriting is the process that an insurer goes through to assign a classification to policy applicants. The assigned classification is based on a number of factors, including your gender, age, hobbies, and medical history. These assignments are based on the underwriting guidelines adopted by the insurer. The better your classification, the lower your premium will be.

The underwriting process is based on an application that you submit, which includes your basic health information, including your exercise, drinking, and smoking habits. It will also delve into your family history regarding a variety of inherited diseases. The insurer will also want to know if you engage in any risky hobbies, such as motorcycle racing, rock climbing, or sky diving. The insurer will likely also require a medical examination, which is paid for by the insurer. The examination may be conducted at a lab, or a medical technician will conduct it in your home or office. If the results of the examination uncover any anomalies, such as high blood pressure or evidence of drug use, then your classification may be reduced or you may be denied coverage entirely. The insurer may also conduct a prescription check, to confirm that the drugs you have listed on the application are the only ones you are currently taking. In addition, the insurer will likely check with the Medical Information Bureau, which is a non-profit trade group that verifies medical information about applicants, in order to avoid fraud.

The underwriting process is conducted by an underwriter, who reviews the data about you and decides whether your composite risk level would be reasonable for the business to insure. In effect, the underwriter is evaluating the risk that you will die during the policy period—which would trigger a payout. This analysis includes checking an actuarial table to estimate your likely remaining lifespan. Actuarial tables can be quite refined, breaking down lifespans by age, gender, and even body mass index. The outcome of this analysis will be your assignment into one of five insurance classification ratings, which are as follows:

- *Preferred plus*. This classification implies that you are in excellent health and have minimal bad habits that might impact your health.
- *Preferred*. This classification implies that you are in good health, but not sufficiently so to qualify for the preferred plus classification. You may have a minor health issue, such as high cholesterol or high blood pressure.
- *Standard plus*. This classification implies that there are some concerns about your medical record, or your family's medical history.
- *Standard*. This classification contains the bulk of all life insurance applicants, and implies that there are clear concerns about your medical record that increase your risk of death.
- *Substandard*. This classification implies that you have a complex medical history that makes you a significantly higher risk to insure.

Tip: If your rating is lower than expected, consider waiting until you are in better health and then applying again. Doing so could save you a substantial amount on your premium payments. Another option is to apply to other insurers, who may assign you a higher rating; this may work when another insurer has a higher risk tolerance for your specific medical condition.

A particular concern is your weight. Insurers may have desired weight ranges for your height, so if you even slightly exceed the weight range for your height, this can automatically drop you into a lower insurance classification.

Another area of concern is tobacco usage, which will undoubtedly raise your premium. Or, if you have quit, then insurers may track the number of years since you have quit. In essence, the risk premium associated with tobacco use declines over time, following your quit date. It is essential to be truthful in reporting your tobacco use to insurers, since some of them will rescind a policy on the grounds of material misrepresentation if you are found to have used tobacco products.

The Conditional Receipt

When you submit a life insurance application to an insurer, it is accompanied by an initial premium payment, from which you receive a *conditional receipt*. This receipt binds your coverage as of the application date, as long as you are deemed eligible for the coverage.

EXAMPLE

Henry applies for $250,000 of life insurance coverage. He is in good health on this date, and receives a conditional receipt. A week later, a palm tree falls over on him in a freak hurricane incident in Florida, killing him. Though the insurer has not yet processed his application, it is obligated to pay his beneficiary the full $250,000 face amount of the policy—once it examines the application and determines that he would have been eligible for the coverage.

EXAMPLE

Charles applies for $400,000 of life insurance coverage and sends in an initial premium payment. At the application date, he is not aware that he has an inoperable brain tumor. He receives a conditional receipt, and undergoes a medical examination the following day. One day later, he dies from a lightning strike while working in his back yard. The medical examination finds that Charles was not eligible for coverage, so the insurer declines the claim and sends the initial premium payment to his beneficiary.

In short, a conditional receipt represents evidence of a preliminary life insurance agreement, which is applicable only until the insurer can conduct its underwriting inquiry and decide whether you are actually eligible for the policy.

Suicide and Incontestability Clause

Most life insurance contracts contain an *incontestability clause*, under which the insurer commits to not contest the contract after a certain period of time has passed—which is usually two years. What this clause is really saying is that the insurer *can* contest the contract during that initial two-year period. The usual reason for a challenge is when the insurer suspects that the applicant lied on his or her initial insurance application. If the insurer finds evidence that the applicant lied, then it can rescind the policy; if so, it must return all premiums paid, along with interest on these funds. In short, it does not pay to lie on an insurance application.

Many policies also contain a suicide clause. This clause allows the insurer to deny claims when the covered party commits suicide within the first year or two of the policy start date. This clause is intended to block anyone who acquires a life insurance policy with the intention of committing suicide in short order, thereby leaving the proceeds to a loved one.

Types of Life Insurance

There are several types of life insurance available. Each one is designed for people with different needs. In the following sub-sections, we examine the characteristics of each type.

Term Life Insurance

Term life insurance is purchased for a specific period of time, after which the policy expires without any residual value. It pays your beneficiaries only if you die during the contract term, and if all required premiums have been paid.

The cost of the policy is lower than for permanent life insurance (which is covered next), since it does not build up any residual cash value. It can be especially inexpensive for younger people, since their odds of death are quite low (see the preceding CDC Life Expectancy Table). Conversely, term life insurance becomes increasingly expensive as you age (and your odds of death increase). Thus, for each successive year during which the policy remains in force, the premium increases to account for the increased probability that you will die.

Tip: If you are contemplating purchasing term life insurance, check the contract details to see how many additional years you can keep renewing the policy, and at what rates.

There are several term life insurance features that can be of use, depending on your situation. They are as follows:

- *Exchange for permanent policy.* Some policies give you the option to convert term insurance into permanent insurance within a specific number of years, even if your health takes a turn for the worse. This can be quite a useful feature in cases where your health is deteriorating, making it difficult to otherwise obtain a new permanent life policy.
- *Annual renewable.* Many policies allow you to keep renewing the policy each year, with a boost in the premium each year. In these policies, the death benefit usually remains the same over time.
- *Level premium.* Some term policies offer a fixed payment amount for a specific number of years, after which any renewal would be at a higher rate.

- *Decreasing term.* Some term policies offer a flat premium, in exchange for a gradual decline in the death benefit. This approach is useful for paying off a mortgage, for which the amount outstanding also declines over time.

Permanent Life Insurance

Permanent life insurance is any life insurance other than term life insurance. This type of insurance generally requires the same premium payment in each year; this is done by mandating higher premiums in the early years of a policy than would be required under a term life policy. The policies will spin off a residual cash value, which you can access with a loan or an outright withdrawal. Further, all earnings on the cash value of the policy are tax-deferred. This approach makes little sense if you do not plan to continue making payments for many years, since there is little (if any) cash accumulation in these policies during their first few years.

Note: The cumulative premiums on permanent life insurance are actually lower than the cumulative premiums on term life insurance if you were to maintain the insurance for your entire life, because the interest income on the residual cash value of the permanent life insurance offsets the higher cost of the life insurance in your later years.

The performance of a permanent life insurance policy is based on four components. The most important performance component is the earnings generated by the insurer in relation to the policy. Clearly, a robustly-performing set of securities and other assets will have a major impact on policy performance. Second is the cost of the life insurance charged by the insurer, which depends on its mortality experience. If its losses are greater than expected, then this will result in a charge against the policy. Third, the insurer will allocate its administrative expenses to the policy. And finally, performance is also derived from the insurer's policy lapse rate. If most of its insured clients continue to pay their premiums, this positively impacts the insurer's costs. All of this can be translated into the following calculation of how the value of a policy is determined:

1. Add the premium paid to the residual value from the end of the preceding period.
2. Subtract mortality costs, administrative costs, and other charges.
3. Add interest, dividends[2], and other earnings

Note: A dividend paid into a life insurance policy is a return of the insurer's surplus to the policy holder. It is essentially a refund of over-charged expenses.

Dividends can be paid out in several ways. One option is for the insurer to pay them out in cash. Since these payments are classified as a return of premiums, they are tax-

---

[2] Dividends are only paid to policies that are designated as participating in dividends. These policies have higher premiums than those that do not participate in dividends, and typically only involve permanent life insurance policies.

free. Another option is to use the dividends to offset any subsequent premium payments; this is an automatic deduction, and so is extremely easy for the policy holder. In cases where dividends are substantial, this can result in the complete elimination of premiums. Yet another possibility is to leave the dividends with the insurer, who will pay interest on these funds; there is usually an option to withdraw the funds as needed. Other options are to use the funds to purchase additional insurance (with no associated commission), and to repay any policy loans that may be outstanding.

Some policies also pay a terminal dividend when they terminate after a minimum period in force, which is usually in the range of 10 to 20 years. This amount can be quite small if a policy is terminated within its first few years of existence, but can be substantial after a number of years have passed.

The interest credit to a policy is the amount that the insurer's investment committee settles upon as being an appropriate payout, based on the firm's earnings on its investment portfolio. This means that policy holders must accept the interest rate declared by the insurer, which may vary from the actual market rate of return. This interest rate is usually applied to the accumulated value of a policy only after all policy expenses have been charged to the policy, which will reduce the accumulated value to which the interest rate is applied – and therefore reduces the amount of interest credited to the policy.

> **Note:** An insurer should disclose to you whether the interest rate being credited to your policy is before any investment and other company expenses have been subtracted, or afterwards.

If the amount of a premium exceeds the net effect of incoming dividends and interest, and outgoing mortality costs and other charges, then this represents an excess cash value for the policy.

It is possible that the premiums you pay for a permanent life insurance policy will change over time, depending on changes in several underlying factors. If the interest rate earnings experienced by the insurer increase, or its mortality experience declines, or its expenses drop, then this can lead to a drop in your premiums. Alternatively, if the insurer's interest rate experience or mortality experience worsens, or if its expenses increase, then these factors can trigger an increase in your premiums.

Examples of several types of permanent life insurance are noted below.

Whole Life Insurance

Under a whole life insurance policy, the insured party makes a standard premium payment for life, after which the face amount is paid to a designated beneficiary. The insurer cannot increase the premium or cancel the policy. However, the policy will lapse if premium payments are not made on time. To mitigate this risk, the policy may allow the insurer to pay for any overdue premium payments from the residual cash value. Several variations on the whole life concept are as follows:

- *Non-participating whole life.* The premium is lower, but the insurer does not pay a regular dividend to the policy holder.
- *Participating whole life.* In exchange for a higher premium, the insurer pays regular dividends to the policy holder. These dividends can take several forms, such as the purchase of additional life insurance, a cash payment, or a reduction in the amount of the next scheduled premium payment.

An ordinary life policy, also known as straight life, is the original whole life insurance concept. It provides for a fixed premium payment over the life of the insured party. The residual cash value increases over the term of the policy, though the cash value is quite low over the first few years of the policy; this is because the agent's commission can easily be half of the first-year premium, if not more.

A variation on the whole life concept is a limited-payment policy, where all premium payments are compressed into a shorter period of time. For example, the policy might be fully paid up by age 50; this approach works well for people who do not want to be burdened with payments following their retirement. Since the payment period is compressed, this also means that the remaining premium payments will be quite high.

Another variation on the concept is indeterminate-premium whole life. Under this arrangement, the insurer sets a maximum premium that it may potentially charge, if it experiences unfavorable mortality, expense, or investment outcomes. The actual premium charged may be well below this figure, in cases where the insurer has experienced better outcomes. The policy may also stipulate that a lower initial rate will be locked in for a period of time, after which the rate may be increased toward the maximum allowable premium.

Yet another variation is the single premium whole life policy. As the name implies, the insured party pays one very large premium at the start of the coverage period, and is done with payments. This policy is not common, since it requires a substantial up-front payment.

Universal Life Insurance

Under a universal life insurance contract, the insured party can alter both the amount and timing of premium payments, as well as the amount of insurance coverage. Under this arrangement, the policy holder is responsible for keeping enough cash in the policy to cover all policy expenses charged by the insurer. As long as this rule is maintained, the policy holder can adjust the timing and amount of payments made. However, the policy can lapse if the policy holder does not make the required minimum payments. These policies suffer from difficult-to-understand periodic reporting by insurers, so that policy holders are unsure of whether their policies are adequately funded.

A complicated version of universal life is equity-indexed universal life. Under this arrangement, a policy has two accounts to which interest income can be credited. One account is associated with a fixed interest rate that the insurer can alter from time to time. The second account is associated with an equity index option that generates returns based on stock market returns. If the stock market returns are negative, then the negative returns are not deducted from the residual cash value of the policy. Many of these policies cap the return that can be generated on the equity index option; this cap provides the insurer with a buffer, which it uses to offset any negative stock market returns.

> **Tip:** See if there is a participation rate associated with your equity-indexed universal life policy. If so, the insurer is keeping a portion of the return from the equity-based portion of the policy. For example, if the market-based return is capped at a 10% return and the participation rate is 70%, then the actual return you will be credited is only 7%.

There are several methods that may be used to calculate the market return for an equity-indexed universal life policy. One is to calculate the average return based on the value of an equity index at the beginning and end of the year, ignoring all changes in-between. Variations on the concept are to calculate the market return based on daily or monthly averages, and compare these amounts to the beginning index value, to see if there has been a gain or a loss.

A potential concern with universal life policies is that many of them terminate the death benefit at age 95 or 100 and cash out at that time. The result is that you receive the cash value of the policy, which may be substantially lower than the death benefit. To avoid this issue, look for policies offering death benefits that continue past age 100.

Variable Life Insurance

Under a variable life insurance contract, the benefits provided by the insurer are not fixed; instead, they vary with the performance of a linked portfolio of investments. The policy holder can select the investments that go into the linked portfolio. One possible outcome of this arrangement is that there are negative returns on the investments; if so, the policy holder may have to pay more funds into the policy in order to keep it in force. Negative returns are more likely when the policy holder chooses an aggressive set of investments that tend to generate more variable returns. Some variable life policies guarantee that death benefits will not fall below a certain minimum threshold, which reduces the effects of negative returns on investment.

> **Tip:** Before signing a variable life contract, review the investment choices, to see if there are options that match your risk profile.

A useful benefit of a variable life policy is that you can surrender it for its residual cash value at any time. In addition, you may have the option to swap out the policy for an annuity contract. However, there are usually substantial policy surrender charges that will be present through the first 10 to 15 years of a policy's life.

> **Tip:** It rarely makes sense to buy a permanent life insurance policy and then surrender it for its cash value after only a few years, given the front-end cost of the salesperson's commission. In these cases, it makes more sense to just purchase term life insurance.

Term Life Insurance Advantages and Disadvantages

There are several advantages to using term life insurance. One is that the premiums are significantly lower than for permanent life insurance. Given the lower price, younger people who presumably have less disposable income are able to afford it. Another advantage is that it can be used for a specific period of time, in order to cover a cash need that spans the same period. For example, life insurance can be purchased that is intended to pay for your mortgage in the event of your death.

There are also several disadvantages to term life insurance. One is that the required premium increases as you age, to reflect the increased risk of your death. Another issue is that coverage ends at the end of the contract term; if you die the next day, there will be no payout. A third concern is that there is no residual cash value associated with a term life policy, so there is no underlying cash asset against which you can borrow funds.

Permanent Life Insurance Advantages and Disadvantages

There are several advantages to using permanent life insurance. First, the policy holder is guaranteed to receive death benefits throughout his or her life, as long as the required premiums are paid. Second, and depending on the policy, the premium amounts can be adjusted over time to match your financial situation. In addition, you can borrow against the cash surrender value of the policy (though this is realistically only a benefit after many years have passed, and the cash surrender value has increased to a reasonable size). Yet another benefit is that it may be possible to surrender the policy and extract the cash surrender value, or flip these funds over into an annuity.

While these are significant advantages, there are also some serious issues with it. One is that premium payments are definitely higher than would be the case with term life insurance; this may limit the amount of life insurance protection that you can afford. This cost difference is substantial, and can be off-putting for someone with limited means.

Term Life vs. Permanent Life Insurance

When contemplating which type of life insurance to acquire, there are several decisions to be made. One of the most important is whether to purchase less-expensive term life insurance, rather than permanent life insurance, and invest the savings. The theory goes that the invested funds and the resulting earnings from them should equal or exceed the residual cash value of a permanent life policy. There is no clear-cut answer to this question. Term life insurance works best when you will only need life insurance for a reduced period of time, while permanent life insurance (as the name implies) is intended to be in effect through the end of your life. For example, someone in his 20s and with a young family probably has little excess cash to spend on permanent life insurance, and so his only realistic option is to buy term life insurance. Conversely, someone later in life who has built up substantial assets might want permanent life insurance, in order to accumulate the residual cash that is a feature of this type of insurance; doing so yields cash that can be used to pay estate taxes. Furthermore, term life insurance is astronomically expensive for people who are more than 70 years old; for them, the only option may be permanent life insurance, which averages out the insurance premium payments over a long period of time. In short, the type of life insurance acquired depends on your specific needs.

The Timing of Premium Payments

The timing and frequency of premium payments can significantly alter the total amount of money that you pay an insurer. The typical insurer wants you to pay a single annual premium, partially to obtain use of the cash as early as possible, and partially to give you fewer decision points at which to decide whether to drop the policy. Consequently, the insurer may charge an additional 4% to 8% if you switch to a monthly payment frequency. This high additional fee is intended to force you into making annual premium payments instead; and if you persist in making monthly payments, then the insurer has just earned an additional profit from this fee.

The concept of premium payment timing is less applicable to universal life policies, since these policies give the policy holder the option to set payment intervals, depending on the contract.

Cash Surrender Value of Permanent Life Insurance

A permanent life insurance policy may have a residual cash value, which is also known as its *cash surrender value*. To calculate this amount, add up all premium payments made into the policy, and then subtract out the fees that the insurer will charge for surrendering the policy. Surrender fees can be extremely high for the first half-decade of a permanent life policy, possibly as much as 100% of the residual cash value. The fees then decline gradually over time, and are usually gone by the 20-year mark.

> **Note:** The average surrender value of a life insurance policy tends to be quite low, frequently in the vicinity of just $500 for every $100,000 of life insurance.

Mortality Charges

There may be a mortality charge against a permanent life insurance policy. This charge is the fee imposed by the insurer to provide life cover to the policy holder. This charge increases as you age, as the risk of death goes up. This charge is based on actuarial experience tables, as well as the insurer's actual mortality experience. These rates can vary substantially by company. For example, a firm that specializes in offering life insurance to heavy smokers will have a much higher mortality rate than one that avoids offering insurance to smokers. The firm with the higher mortality rate will therefore apply a significantly higher mortality charge against the accounts of its policy holders.

The costs of anticipated death claims are generally about three-quarters of the costs associated with any life insurance policy, so mortality estimates and actual experiences by the insurer have a major impact on the costs charged against its policy holders.

Insurer Expenses

An insurance company is subject to an array of expenses. A significant one is sales expenses, including commissions, sales offices, and marketing expenditures. In the first year that a policy is in force, a major expense is the associated salesperson commission. This commission can equal or even exceed the amount of all first-year premiums, after which it declines to a more modest commission in succeeding years – typically in the range of 2-10%.

There are also fees associated with the premiums paid into an insurance policy. State premium taxes are a percentage of the premiums paid by insured parties. The maximum state premium tax is 4%, while the most common percentage is 2.5%.

These premium-related expenses may be more heavily charged against a permanent life policy early in its term, so that the insurer recovers its costs as soon as possible. Later on, these charges are greatly reduced, when only policy administration expenses are still being incurred by the insurer.

> **Note:** When the disclosures associated with a policy show unusually low charges that will be levied against a policy, there is a good chance that the insurer is making up the difference by crediting a lower interest rate to accounts, or by charging a higher mortality rate.

Policy Loans

Certain types of permanent life insurance permit *policy loans*, which means that you can borrow money from the residual cash value on your policy. This is not exactly a loan, since there is no requirement to pay back the borrowed funds, though you will need to pay interest. This is really more of an advance of the funds that the insurer would eventually have been obligated to pay you anyways—the payment date is merely being advanced. In many cases, policy holders take out policy loans in order to fund the ongoing premiums on their policies.

While this can be a useful source of cash, be aware that there are also some serious risks associated with policy loans, which are as follows:

- *Premature policy lapse*. If the residual cash value of a policy is drawn down by a loan, then the risk of a policy lapse increases. Consequently, you must weigh whether it makes sense to take out a loan against a policy when doing so could result in you having no coverage at all.

- *Taxable income.* There are situations in which the interest on a policy loan is not deductible, though the requirements are complex.
- *Over-loaning.* A policy holder might take loans against a policy in order to pay the annual premium on it. At some point, it will no longer be financially tenable to keep paying interest on the loan, while the net death benefit of the policy becomes vanishingly small. At this point, the policy holder may need to surrender the policy and also pay a taxable gain (which is calculated as the gross proceeds from the policy in the form of the net surrender value plus the loan amount outstanding, minus the basis in the policy).

In short, it can be quite dangerous to take out a policy loan, especially when the intent is to use the funds to pay for ongoing premiums. Doing so should only be a short-term solution to maintaining a policy, and should only be done with the advice of a knowledgeable agent.

Premium Financing

Under a premium financing arrangement, a lender pays the premiums on a life insurance policy, under the understanding that the lender will be paid back from the death benefit. This approach can work well when interest rates are low, since the lender is paid off and there is still some residual cash left over for the beneficiaries. However, there are several concerns with these arrangements. First, the loan is usually intended to last for only a decade or so, which means that the policy holder must be within 10 years of his or her end of life before entering into the arrangement—at which point the insurance will be exceedingly expensive. Second, the interest rate associated with the loan could increase over time, which may wipe out any benefits that the beneficiaries might otherwise realize from the arrangement. Third, the lender will require that collateral be posted against the loan, usually in the form of the cash surrender value on the policy. However, if this is not sufficient (such as when the value of the collateral declines), then other collateral will need to be posted—potentially resulting in a number of collateral calls that could slowly wipe out the assets of the insured party. And finally, the lender might not choose to keep extending the loan, in which case the policy holder will need to come up with sufficient cash to pay off the loan balance.

No-Load Life Insurance

Most life insurance is sold with a commission built into the premium structure. That is, you do not see the commission, because it is being taken from your initial premium payments. A variation on the concept is no-load life insurance, where your insurance advisor is being compensated on a separate fee basis. A no-load policy can be a good idea, since paying a separate, up-front fee keeps a commission from being extracted from the earliest premium payments, allowing residual cash values on permanent life policies to grow more quickly.

Useful Policy Riders

A policy rider is a contract addendum that provides you with an added benefit beyond what is specified in the main insurance contract, or a reduced benefit. There are a variety of policy riders available, including the following:

- *Accelerated death benefit.* This rider triggers a payout if the insured party is diagnosed with a terminal illness. A variation is the terminal benefits rider, which is designed for people with terminal illnesses; they can collect part of their life insurance early, in order to pay for their ongoing care.
- *Cost-of-living benefit.* This rider allows you to buy additional life insurance without evidence of insurability, in an amount equaling the percentage change in the consumer price index.
- *Disability benefit.* This rider pays out a fraction of the death benefit, if you are permanently disabled.
- *Other insured benefit.* This rider provides coverage to one or more additional parties. A variation is the spousal rider, which provides coverage to your spouse.
- *Waiver of premium benefit.* This rider provides a waiver of all remaining premium payments, if you become totally and permanently disabled.

Keep in mind that an insurer would not offer these riders unless they were profitable, so consider the matter carefully before purchasing one.

Tax Implications of Life Insurance

Generally, the proceeds from a life insurance policy are not subject to taxation. However, the proceeds are then combined with the other assets in the beneficiary's estate, and are then subject to estate taxation. If the total net assets of the estate exceed the minimum threshold at which estate tax begins to apply, then estate tax will apply to the amount of assets that exceed this minimum threshold. Outside of these general rules, there are some other situations that can impact income taxes, including the following:

- *Policy is surrendered at a loss.* If the policy holder surrenders the policy, and the aggregate amount of cash value and dividends is less than the total premiums paid, then there is a loss. This loss is not deductible.
- *Policy is surrendered at a gain.* If the policyholder surrenders the policy, and the aggregate amount of cash value and dividends is greater than the total premiums paid, then there is a gain. This gain is normally treated as ordinary income to the taxpayer.

Transferring Policy Ownership

In those rare cases in which your estate is large enough to be subject to the federal estate tax, it can make sense to transfer the ownership of your life insurance policies to another party. If you own or have any control[3] over the policy at the time of your death, then the proceeds from the insurance are included in the calculation of your estate. Conversely, if policy ownership can be shifted elsewhere, then the proceeds are not included in your estate.

> **Note:** If the policy proceeds are payable to your spouse, then they are not subject to the federal estate tax.

Transferring policy ownership is allowable, as long as the insurer has a record of the transfer (usually on one of its own transfer forms, specifying that the insured party is no longer the owner). You can assign ownership to any adult, which may include the beneficiary of the policy. However, you will lose all control over the policy once it has been transferred, so you will no longer be able to cancel the policy or alter the beneficiary. Consequently, it makes the most sense to only transfer the ownership of a life insurance policy to someone you trust implicitly.

> **Tip:** If you are going to transfer ownership of a life insurance policy, do it while you are still healthy, since the IRS will disallow the transfer if it occurs within three years of your death.

The act of transferring a life insurance policy to someone else creates a taxable gift. This means that a gift tax will be assessed on the present value of the policy, subject to the current gift tax rules. This is still likely to be a good deal, since the proceeds to be gained from the policy are usually far less when you are alive than the much larger payout after you have died.

EXAMPLE

Andrea transfers the ownership of her life insurance policy to her daughter Willie. On the day she authorizes the transfer, the cash surrender value of the policy is $35,000. Andrea dies five years later, at which point the insurer pays Willie $500,000, which is the policy payout. Neither amount is included in Andrea's estate, and Willie pays taxes on the cash surrender value of the policy.

The downside for the person receiving the gift of an insurance policy is that this person should now make all scheduled premium payments. Otherwise, if you were to keep

---

[3] You are considered to still have control over a life insurance policy if you can cancel it, change the beneficiary, borrow against it, or change the manner in which policy payments are made.

making payments, then the IRS could make a strong case that you still control the policy, so the policy payout should be included in your estate.

Irrevocable Life Insurance Trust

If you have a life insurance policy, then the proceeds from it will be included in the valuation of your estate when you die. If the policy is for a large amount, this may mean that some estate tax will be owed. To avoid estate tax, consider including the policy in an irrevocable life insurance trust. As the name implies, you will have no control over the trust once it has been set up, which also means that you cannot be trustee. This trust owns the life insurance policy, so the proceeds from the policy are excluded from your estate. Instead, the proceeds are paid out to the designated beneficiaries. This can be a particularly useful approach when the beneficiary is a minor, in which case the trustee can be instructed to maintain control over the funds until the minor becomes an adult.

There are legal fees associated with the creation of an irrevocable life insurance trust, so this may not be a cost-effective option when the amount of insurance placed in the trust is small.

EXAMPLE

George is the widowed father of two daughters, neither of whom has any sense with money. He has a whole life insurance policy that will pay out $3 million when he dies, as well as millions in other assets. He wants to minimize his estate taxes while also ensuring that the daughters do not spend the money coming from the insurance policy in a profligate manner. George asks a trusted friend to be the trustee of a life insurance trust, to which he transfers the policy. Following George's death, the friend will administer the money for his daughters in accordance with George's wishes, as stated in the trust documentation.

A life insurance trust is only considered valid by the IRS if you are not the trustee, it is irrevocable (you can't revoke it), and it was established at least three years prior to your death. Otherwise, the IRS will disregard the existence of the trust and assume that the life insurance proceeds are part of your estate.

Policy Cost Comparisons

A common question is how to compare the cost of different life insurance policies. This is relatively easy for term life insurance; as long as the coverage amounts and policy term periods are the same on several comparison policies, then the only remaining variable left to examine is the premium amount. In this comparison, be sure to use comparable policy term periods; this refers to the number of years that premiums remain at the current level. An additional consideration is the financial stability of the insurance provider. There are several credit rating agencies, such as AM Best, that provide insurer ratings.

Cost comparisons are more difficult for permanent life insurance policies, since they contain so many more variables. For these policies, and in addition to the comparisons already noted, you can examine the availability of insurance riders, whether these policies can be converted into other insurance products, the size of surrender fees, and how long before surrender fees are phased out. Some policies build up residual cash values, while others do not. Furthermore, some policies allow you to convert to an alternative form of insurance, while others do not. Given the variety of variables, comparisons of permanent life policies tend to be more qualitative in nature.

One way to examine the "innards" of a life insurance policy is to examine the associated life insurance illustration in detail. A *life insurance illustration* is a presentation of how a policy should perform under certain circumstances.[4] These illustrations can differ somewhat by policy type, but there are many common elements, such as the benefits provided, the premiums required, the expenses related to a policy, and the benefit and premium periods. The intent of an illustration is to ensure that a purchaser is not misled, and to make the presented information more understandable.

There are three types of life insurance illustration. There is a basic illustration, a supplemental illustration, and an in-force illustration. By using uniform presentations in these illustrations, customers can more easily compare the policies being offered by different insurers. A basic illustration shows the guaranteed and non-guaranteed parts of the policy. Guaranteed policy elements include death benefits, premiums, credits, and charges. For example, the illustration might state that the initial death benefit is $1,000,000, with an initial premium of $750, which is guaranteed to be renewable until age 90. Non-guaranteed policy elements include current death benefits, fund accumulations, and cash value. The basic illustration presents this information in a narrative summary and numeric summary, with accompanying tabular data. A supplemental illustration shows only the non-guaranteed elements stated in the basic illustration; it gives the insurer more flexibility for explaining how its insurance product works. An *in-force illustration* is provided periodically after the first policy anniversary, and is presented in the same format as the basic illustration. It employs actual values and uses the most current assumptions, such as the current mortality and expense factors, and so gives you the best possible view of policy performance. It is also useful for determining the minimum premium needed to ensure that the policy will continue to its maturity date.

> **Note:** You may need to request an in-force illustration, as many insurers do not voluntarily issue them. The problem is that, once a policy is sold, there is little to no interaction with the agent who sold it, leaving no one to monitor the performance of the policy—other than the policy holder.

It is entirely possible that the initial assumptions and premium amount associated with a policy are no longer valid, typically due to increases in the insurer's mortality

---

[4] The guidelines for life insurance illustrations are developed by the National Association of Insurance Commissioners, and may (or may not) be adopted for use by each individual State Department of Insurance.

charges and other expenses. If so, you will need to make increased premium payments (perhaps substantially so) in order to reach your targeted policy value. This is a particular concern when you have taken policy loans against the policy (see the prior Policy Loans section).

The Selection of a Life Insurance Company

It is essential to have an understanding of the life insurance company from which you plan to purchase a life insurance product, since it is possible for one of these entities to fail, potentially leaving you with reduced or no coverage.

A life insurance company is usually organized as either a stock company or a mutual company. A stock company is owned by shareholders, who elect a board of directors that oversees the activities of management. Conversely, a mutual insurance company has no shareholders. Instead, policy owners are considered to be its owners. This means that the insurer may return some of its excess earnings to its policy holders as dividends. There is an ongoing trend of demutualizing, where mutual insurance companies are converting into stock companies. Generally, a stock company has more sources of financing, since they can sell shares, while a mutual company can only issue debt or borrow from policyholders. This does not necessarily mean that a stock company is always more financially stable—only that it has a greater opportunity to *be* stable.

The best single source of information about the financial stability of a life insurance company is its credit rating. This rating may be provided by one or more of the following credit rating agencies:

- *AM Best Company*. This agency has the most experience rating insurance companies. Its ratings cover the insurer as a whole, and not individual insurance products. Its Financial Strength Rating (FRS) represents the firm's opinion about an insurer's ability to meet its policy-related obligations.
- *Fitch Ratings*. This is a smaller rating agency, and is not as focused specifically on insurers. Its rating process is more similar to the following two agencies than to the AM Best methodology.
- *Moody's Investors Services*. This agency is more broad-based, providing ratings for businesses in all industries. As such, it may not provide ratings for a particular insurer. It ranks insurers according to a creditworthiness scale, which means that it weighs the outstanding debts and other financial risks of insurers.
- *Standard and Poor's*. This agency is more broad-based, providing ratings for businesses in all industries. As such, it may not provide ratings for a particular insurer. Its Insurer Financial Strength Rating is a forward-looking opinion about an insurer's ability to pay its policies and contracts.

Each of these agencies employs a somewhat different rating system, so they may produce somewhat different ratings for the same insurer. The system employed will likely include an analysis of some mix of financial stability, debt leverage, management stability, short-term financial performance, and level of diversification. A comparison of the rating systems used by the four agencies appears in the following exhibit.

Credit Rating Comparison

Risk Level	AM Best	Fitch	Moody's	Standard & Poor's
Investment grade:				
(highest investment grade)	A++	AAA	Aaa	AAA
	A+	AA+	Aa1	AA+
	A	AA	Aa2	AA
	A-	AA-	Aa3	AA-
	B++	A+	A1	A+
	B+	A	A2	A
	B	A-	A3	A-
	B-	BBB+	Baa1	BBB+
	C++	BBB	Baa2	BBB
(lowest investment grade)	C+	BBB-	Baa3	BBB-
Speculative grade:				
(highest speculative grade)	C	BB+	Ba1	BB+
	C-	BB	Ba2	BB
	D	BB-	Ba3	BB-
	E	B+	B1	B+
	F	B	B2	B
		B-	B3	B-
		CCC+	Caa1	CCC+

Note: There are additional lower speculative grades than those listed in this table.

We will focus for a moment on a few of the AM Best ratings, since they are most directly applicable to insurers. Their top rating is A++, which represents a superior ability to meet all obligations to policy holders. Insurers with ratings extending down as far as a B+ rating are probably reasonable entities from which to purchase insurance, though insurers as close to the A++ rating are your best bet. Below the B+ rating, it is increasingly likely that insurers will have trouble meeting their financial obligations. Those with an E rating have been placed under regulatory supervision, while those with an F rating are currently under liquidation proceedings.

None of the ratings provided by the credit rating agencies can be considered a direct recommendation to purchase a specific policy (or not). However, these ratings can be quite useful for evaluating the overall financial viability of an insurer.

> **Tip:** After you have selected a policy offered by an insurer, it makes sense to continue monitoring the credit ratings assigned to the insurer – perhaps on an annual basis. By tracking these ratings on a trend line, you can spot declines in financial condition, as per the analysis of the applicable rating agency.

Insurer Bankruptcy

What happens if a life insurance company goes bankrupt? The bankruptcy is overseen by the insurance department of the state in which it is located. There is also a state guaranty association, which provides coverage, up to a set limit (which may vary by state), for the holders of policies issued by the bankrupt entity. A common guarantee for life insurance death benefits is $300,000, while the guarantee for the cash surrender value of a policy is $100,000. This association also reviews the commitments of the entity, verifies that covered claims are made, and arranges for all remaining policies to be shifted over to another insurer that is willing to take them on.

When the bankrupt entity is located in more than one state, the bankruptcy is overseen by the National Association of Life and Health Insurance Guaranty Associations, which coordinates the activities of the state-level organizations.

Ongoing Life Insurance Reviews

Once you have an approved life insurance policy in place, this does not mean that you should ignore it from that point forward. In the case of a permanent life insurance policy, you should certainly review it every few years, in light of your changing circumstances. It is entirely possible that you will need to alter the face amount of the policy, thereby adjusting the amount that your beneficiary eventually receives. Or, you may wish to alter the nature of the policy, perhaps switching to a whole life policy or term life policy. Further, it may be worthwhile to see if any riders you have been paying for are still necessary. If not, they can be withdrawn from the contract, thereby reducing the amount of the premium. And finally, you may want to consider whether the primary and contingent beneficiaries are still the parties that you want to have receive the policy payout.

Policy Replacement Options

There may be cases in which it makes sense to replace a life insurance policy with another one. A good argument can be made for such a replacement when your original policy was based on you being in a lower insurance classification, and your health now warrants placement in a higher classification (resulting in lower premiums). For example, you might have quit smoking several years ago, which extends your projected lifespan. Another good reason for a switch is when the insurer's financial condition has clearly declined in the intervening years. Or, the costs charged against your current policy are excessive when compared to the charges applied to other policies today.

However, there are also disadvantages to replacing your policy. One is certainly that a large sales commission will be extracted from your first-year premium on the new policy. Also, the incontestability clause will start afresh, so the insurer will be able to contest whether the policy is valid for the first two years. Yet another concern is when your health has declined since the original policy was issued, since this can land you in a lower insurance classification (resulting in higher premiums). These are important disadvantages, especially the large commission charge. Consequently, it is generally not a good idea to replace a life insurance policy.

> **Tip:** Do not replace a policy because the original one did not provide sufficient coverage. Instead, just buy additional insurance that will incrementally provide the additional amount that you need.

Determining the Amount of an Insurance Payout

When an insured party dies, the amount that the insurer pays out (if at all) will depend on the circumstances. Here are several common situations:

- *Term life insurance.* The face amount will be paid, as long as the insured party died while the policy was still in force.
- *Permanent life insurance.* The face amount will be paid, as long as the policy is designed to borrow from the residual cash value in order to pay premiums. If no premiums are paid and there is no residual cash value from which to borrow, then there will be no payout. Or, the insurer may keep the policy in force, but reduce the total amount of the payout.

Obtaining a Claim Payout

In order to obtain a payout on a life insurance policy, the beneficiary should have ready access to the associated life insurance policy. Using the identification and contact information on this policy, contact the life insurance company to request a claim form. The insurer will also need a copy of the death certificate. In cases where the insurance was placed through an employer plan, contact the employer's human resources department for assistance in filing the claim.

The insured party might have already chosen a method of payment for the payout. Alternatively, the insurer may leave this choice up to the beneficiary. In the latter case, the choices are for the insurer to pay out a lump sum payment, or to park the funds in a money market account and issue a checkbook to the beneficiary, or to issue a series of payments as an income annuity, or to only pay out interest, with the principal eventually going to a secondary beneficiary.

These payouts are usually made quite soon after the death of the insured party. However, if the death occurred within two years of the policy issuance date, then expect some delays while the insurer investigates to see if it can challenge the claim due to fraudulent information on the policy application.

> **Tip:** If you suspect that you might be the designated beneficiary on someone's life insurance policy, go through their cancelled checks for at least the last 12 months, to see if they made any payments to an insurance company. Another option is to review their bank records for electronic payments. Yet another option is to review their last tax return for interest income or interest expenses related to permanent life insurance policies.

Life Insurance Industry Issues

There are a few business issues to be aware of that impact the economics of the life insurance industry. They are noted in the following sub-sections.

Policyholder Volume

From the perspective of the insurer, it is essential to increase the number of life insurance policyholders. When there are many policyholders, the insurer can be more confident in its prediction of how many policyholders will die in any given year. Conversely, if the number of policyholders were quite small, there would be an increased risk of an unexpectedly large payout occurring.

Persistency

A central issue for many insurers is *persistency*, which is how long their policies remain active. Many permanent life insurance policy holders allow their policies to lapse, which translates into a lower level of persistency. When many policies lapse early, this may be prior to when the insurer has been able to offset all of its costs against premiums (which can take more than a decade to accomplish). If this happens, the insurer must absorb the excess costs. When there are many of these lapses, an insurer will have a hard time consistently earning a profit.

An insurer can create a policy product that deliberately charges off all expenses against the policy in its first year, which allows the insurer to start reporting a profit on it much sooner than normal. You can detect these situations by examining the associated life insurance illustration to determine how long it takes for the cash surrender value to exceed the sum of all premiums paid. If it takes less than 10 years for this threshold to be reached, it is likely that the insurer is charging off all policy-related expenses at an accelerated rate.

> **Note:** Persistency is more of a problem when the insurer pays the bulk of the related sales commission up-front, since there is no incentive for salespeople to encourage clients to continue paying their premiums. Conversely, a more spread-out compensation plan tends to reduce the persistency issue.

Life Reinsurance

Life reinsurance occurs when an insurer shifts some of the risk associated with a life insurance policy to a reinsurer. The reinsurer accepts this risk in exchange for a fee, and agrees to reimburse the primary insurer for the portion of any claim that was originally reinsured against. Doing so spreads out the risk of loss, since a large claim must now be paid out by several insurers. This approach is most commonly taken when a significant portion of an insurer's business could be at risk due to a similar loss event. For example, an insurer whose clients are mostly located in a single flood plain might reinsure some of the risk, in case a single flooding event kills a number of customers who reside within the flood plain.

Life reinsurance is also a good idea when an insurer wants to increase its capacity to take on new clients. For example, an insurer might spot an opportunity to sell life insurance at unusually high premiums in the Arizona region, due to inattention by competing life insurance companies. Accordingly, it reinsures the bulk of its life insurance in the Florida market, allowing it to write more insurance business in the Arizona market.

Accounting for Business-Owned Life Insurance

A business may own life insurance that covers its owners or key employees. If term life insurance is purchased, then the accounting is quite simple; just recognize the expense over the coverage period.

EXAMPLE

Failsafe Containment purchases key man insurance on one of its executives who is deeply involved in its product development process. The policy premium is $12,000, and provides $1 million of life insurance for one year. The initial payment is recorded as an increase in the prepaid expenses asset account, with the following entry:

	Debit	Credit
Prepaid expenses [asset]	12,000	
Cash [asset]		12,000

During the first month of the coverage period, Failsafe charges $1/12^{th}$ of the prepaid expense to expense, using the following entry:

	Debit	Credit
Insurance expense [expense]	1,000	
Prepaid expenses [asset]		1,000

By the end of the 12-month period, all of the prepaid expense will have been charged to expense.

The accounting situation is more complex if the business purchases a permanent life insurance policy instead. In this case, the accounting standards mandate that the owning organization record an asset at the amount that could be realized under the insurance contract at the financial statement date. However, an asset is only realized when the asset is controlled by the company and will provide it with a future economic benefit. Therefore, if the proceeds from the policy are going to the employee in question, then this is actually just a benefit expense; if so, the accounting is simply to charge all premium payments to expense. It is an open question as to whether the expense account charged should be insurance expense or benefits expense. In the following example, we assume that the expense is charged to the insurance expense account.

EXAMPLE

Giro Cabinetry purchases a permanent life insurance contract on its owner, where the annual premium is $20,000. The owner controls the cash surrender value of the policy, and the death benefit is assigned to his wife, who is the primary beneficiary. Since the company gains no economic benefit from this arrangement, the entire amount of the payment is charged to expense as incurred, as noted in the following journal entry:

	Debit	Credit
Insurance expense [expense]	20,000	
Cash [asset]		20,000

What about cases in which the business controls the life insurance asset and will be provided by it with a future economic benefit? The death benefit proceeds can be considered a future economic benefit, though there is great uncertainty about when the insured party will die, and whether the policy will remain in force. Given this uncertainty, it is not possible to recognize the death benefit until it is actually received. However, the cash surrender value of the policy provides a future economic benefit, since it is the amount that can be realized if the policy is surrendered—and this is an amount that can be readily calculated. Therefore, the business records the initial cash surrender value of the policy, and then adjusts this recorded value over time, as the underlying cash surrender value also changes. The difference between the premiums paid during the reporting period and any increase in the cash surrender value is recorded as insurance expense. Towards the end of the policy period, the increase in cash surrender value could very well be greater than the amount of the premium paid, in which case the difference is reported as income. Once the insured party dies, the company receives the policy proceeds from the insurer. The excess of this payout over the amount recorded as an asset is reported as income, while the life insurance asset is removed from the balance sheet.

EXAMPLE

Prickly Corporation takes out a $500,000 permanent life insurance policy on its founder. The initial annual payment is for $16,000, which is recorded as follows:

	Debit	Credit
Insurance expense [expense]	10,000	
Cash surrender value [asset]	6,000	
Cash [asset]		16,000

Years later, the cash surrender value of the policy has grown to $150,000, at which point the founder dies and the company receives the $500,000 death benefit. The resulting entry is:

	Debit	Credit
Cash [asset]	500,000	
Cash surrender value [asset]		150,000
Gain on insurance proceeds [income]		350,000

Summary

Life insurance can be a valuable part of anyone's lifetime financial plan. However, the need for it changes over time, so you should examine it in relation to your financial circumstances and lifetime goals on a periodic basis. Furthermore, if you are using permanent life insurance products, be aware that their values can veer off in unexpected directions over time, so review them periodically to ensure that they are still sufficient to fulfill your financial planning needs.

Glossary

B

Beneficiary. The party that will receive the payout from a policy's death benefit when the policy holder dies.

C

Cash surrender value. The amount payable if a life insurance policy is surrendered.

Conditional receipt. A receipt from an insurer that binds coverage as of the application date, as long as the applicant is deemed eligible for the coverage.

D

Death benefit. The payout from a life insurance policy that your beneficiaries will receive in the event of your death.

I

Incontestability clause. A contract clause under which the insurer commits to not contest the contract after a certain period of time has passed.

Insurable interest. An economic stake in an event for which someone purchases an insurance policy to mitigate the risk of loss.

Interest rate. The rate credited to a policy by the insurer, which is applied to the accumulation value as reduced by any policy loans.

L

Life insurance. An insurance product that pays out a designated amount of cash upon the death of an insured person.

Life reinsurance. When an insurer shifts some of the risk associated with a life insurance policy to a reinsurer.

M

Mortality charge. The fee imposed by the insurer to provide life cover to the policy holder.

P

Permanent life insurance. Any life insurance other than term life insurance.

Persistency. How long an insurer's policies remain active.

Policy loan. An amount borrowed against the accumulated value of a permanent life insurance policy.

Premium financing. When a lender pays the premiums on a life insurance policy, under the understanding that the lender will be paid back from the death benefit.

S

Surrender charge. The fee charged by the insurer if you elect to terminate a policy early. This charge declines as a policy ages.

T

Term insurance. Insurance that is purchased for a specific period of time, after which the policy expires without any residual value.

U

Underwriting. The process that an insurer goes through to assign a classification to policy applicants.

Universal life insurance. When the insured party can alter both the amount and timing of premium payments, as well as the amount of insurance coverage.

V

Variable life insurance. When the benefits provided by the insurer are not fixed; instead, they vary with the performance of a linked portfolio of investments.

Viatical settlement. When terminally ill policy holders sell their policies for a percent of the death benefit.

W

Whole life insurance. When the insured party makes a standard premium payment for life, after which the face amount is paid to a designated beneficiary.

Index